GRAMERCY GREAT MASTERS

Acknowledgments

The publishers would like to thank the museums for reproduction permission and in particular the **BRIDGEMAN ART LIBRARY** and **SCALA Istituto Fotografico Editoriale** for their help in supplying the illustrations for the book.

Board of Trustees of the V. & A.: Marcelle Lender Dancing the Bolero in Chilpéric, May Milton; The Jockey; Aristide Bruant at les Ambassadeurs; Poster for the Divan Japonais.

British Library, London: May Belfort; May Belfort (lithograph).

Christie's, London: Woman in a Corset from "Elles"; Femme au Tub; Au Moulin Rouge: La Goulue et sa Sœur; Napoleon.

Glyptoflek, Copenhagen: Portrait of Suzanne Valadon.

Kunsthaus, Zurich: At the Bar, the Client and the Cashier.

Hussmann, Zurich: The Sphinx.

Los Angeles County Museum of Arts: Messalina Descending the Staircase.

Louvre, Paris: Jane Avril Dancing.

Musée d'Orsay, Paris: Woman Putting on Her Stockings; The Clowness Cha-Wo-Kao.

Musée des Augustins, Toulouse: Woman at Her Toilet.

Musée Toulouse-Lautrec, Albi: The Englishwoman at "The Star"; Madame Poupoule at Her Dressing Table; Examination at the Faculty of Medicine; Self-Portrait; Young Routy at Céleyran; Portrait of the Artist's Mother at Breakfast; Jardin de Paris: Jane Avril; Loïe Fuller; Yvette Guilbert Greeting Her Audience; The Salon in the Rue des Moulins.

Museum of Fine Arts, Budapest: In the Moulin Rouge; Moulin Rouge.

Philadelphia Museum of Art: Dancing at the Moulin Rouge: La Goulue and Valentin le Désossé.

National Gallery, London: Woman Sitting in a Garden.

Private Collection: May Belfort; Portrait of Oscar Wilde; Study for a Box at the Theater; Jane Avril; Reine de Joie; Aristide Bruant dans son Cabaret; La Chaîne Simpson.

Victoria & Albert Museum, London: (Moulin Rouge) La Goulue.

Published by Gramercy Books
distributed by Random House Value Publishing, Inc.
40 Engelhard Avenue
Avenel, New Jersey 07001

Printed and bound in Italy

ISBN: 0-517-12404-1

10 9 8 7 6 5 4 3 2 1

Toulouse-Lautrec

GRAMERCY BOOKS

NEW YORK • AVENEL

Toulouse-Lautrec
His Life and Works

ORIGINS OF THE MOULIN ROUGE

Eighteen eighty-nine was an important year for France. The great steel tower more than 980 feet tall built by Gustave Eiffel for the Centennial Exposition promised a brilliant industrial future. The defeat of 1870 had been forgotten, and an industrious optimism was spreading everywhere. On October 5, a new nightclub was opened in Montmartre, at 50 Boulevard de Clichy: the "Moulin Rouge" dance hall.

For the city, it was love at first sight: those fascinating, enticingly clothed amazons met with unprecedented success. In place of the popular dance hall "Reine Blanche" the brilliant impresario Charles Zidler had built a dream machine! The newspapers wrote of a "very Parisian show, which husbands can come to see together with their wives." While this was not strictly true, Zidler and his partner Oller were not really pulling the wool over their patrons' eyes — or at least not the husbands'. The vast dance hall was reached through a long gallery lined with red wallpaper and decorated with paintings, posters and photographs.

This is where Toulouse-Lautrec was to hold his first exhibition, and it was here that he would always find inspiration and material for his paintings. Indeed, Montmartre, the Moulin Rouge and its cancan dancers are virtually synonymous with the name of Lautrec. An observant and accurate witness of that *fin-de-siècle* world, he was better placed than anyone else to draw the secret truth of the human condition from fleeting images of an ever precarious life.

In his depictions, the light is dazzling and plentiful: shining brass fixtures underscore the thrusts of the dancers whirling gaily in their skirts full of tucks and frills. Professional dancers take turns with singers and acrobats, and during the breaks the public takes over the room, while the artists who have finished their acts sit with customers at the tables surrounding the dance floor.

To the left of the entrance are the *cocottes*, sitting at the tables, smiling and always ready for a drink. Others stroll around the room and through the gallery. Outside, in the garden, just as brightly lit, the scene is very similar: the orchestra playing loudly and noisily for the cancan dancing. A few tame monkeys chase each other among the chairs to the onlookers' amusement. An enormous wooden elephant, like the wooden horse of Troy, hides other surprises inside it: an orchestra, girls disguised as Moors who specialized in belly dancing; and the most famous and "finest" of all the attractions, the great Pétomane.

The bills posted around the city describe every detail of the spiciest aspects of the attractions of the Moulin Rouge, this "High-Life Rendez-Vous." In order to make it easier to attract patrons, Charles Zidler decided to exploit a new form of advertising: the colored posters of which Toulouse-Lautrec was to become the inimitable master.

Duke Élie de Talleyrand, Prince De Sagan, Prince Troubetzkoi, and Count La Rochefoucauld were fervent patrons, and their enthusiasm brought the whole French aristocracy flocking to the Moulin Rouge. Foreigners passing through Paris, too, felt it their (pleasant) duty to spend their evenings at the Moulin Rouge. Even the Prince of Wales, the future Edward VII, *arbiter elegantiarum*, made a few brief appearances in an attempt to forget the excessively strict protocol of the courts.

HENRI'S YOUTH

Henri de Toulouse-Lautrec, one of the liveliest, most independent and rebellious artistic talents of his time, enlivened the artistic scene in Paris in the years immediately after Impressionism.

Henri-Marie-Raymond de Toulouse-Lautrec-Monfa was born on the night of November 24, 1864, at the Hôtel du Bosc in Albi. He was the son of two first cousins, descendants of two of the oldest and noblest families of the French aristocracy.

His father, the refined and bizarre Count Alphonse-Charles-Marie de Toulouse-Lautrec-Monfa, whose surname had become famous as far back as the crusades, divided his time between the wordly delights of Paris life and hunting on his vast estates.

Henri's mother, Countess Adèle-Zoë-Marie-Marquette Tapié de Céleyran, on the other hand, was a woman of sound principles, profoundly religious, both gentle and strict at the same time. It was she who always represented a safe haven for Henri, where he could find refuge from the difficulties of life and the support he needed in times of crisis.

Portrait of Carmen

Henri spent his early years on the family's estates in the Viaur valley (thirty miles from Albi) and in Céleyran. Then, in 1868 his brother, Richard, died at the age of one, and from that time on his parents lived apart.

In 1872 Countess Adèle and Henri went to live in Paris. At first they lived in the Pérey building in Rue Boissy d'Anglas, then in Neuilly. On October 1 Henri started school, with excellent results, at the prestigious Lycée Fontanes (the future Condorcet), together with his cousins Louis Pascal and Maurice Joyant, who was to become his best friend, his art dealer and his biographer. In Henri's exercise books, English and Latin translations mingled increasingly with rapidly drawn sketches. Caricatures of his teachers and relatives and sketches of horses bore witness even then, if not to a vocation, at least to a strong penchant for pencils and paintbrushes. Perhaps this bent would never have gone beyond the limits of a leisure activity (among his ancestors painting was a favorite hobby) had it not been for ill health and two unfortunate accidents, one shortly after the other. These misfortunes suddenly upset the life of this young man, forcing him into a very different type of existence from that to which he seemed destined by birth and by character.

First, he was forced by his frail health to leave school and continue his studies at home, at Albi. Then, on May 30, 1878, in Albi, while getting up from a low chair, he slipped on the floor of the hall and fractured his left thighbone. Convalescing after a long spell in bed, he visited the spa at Barèges, near Amélie-les-Bains. In August of the following year, during another period at Barèges, he had a nasty fall into a ditch while taking a walk, and he fractured his right thighbone, too.

By that time he was fated. The long and exhausting ordeal of operations, cures and spas left him with the certainty that his injured legs would never grow. Tied to his bed for long periods, he felt deprived of the things he loved most. Unable to play games and run in the open air, tortured by physical suffering, humiliated by the awareness of his deformities, Henri reacted to the cruelty of his fate with surprising strength of mind. He discovered that drawing provided him with a tool that could help him overcome the loneliness and boredom of long hours of immobility. Thus, encouraged by René Princeteau, a deaf-and-dumb painter friend of Count Alphonse, he asked to be allowed to devote himself to art.

Drawing soon became a great passion. Still a weak youth, he spent almost all of 1880 drawing and painting, interspersed by brief convalescent stays in Nice, Céleyran and Albi. To please his mother, Henri decided to resume his studies. But in July 1881, in Paris, he failed his graduation exams. He had to repeat them in Toulouse in November of the same year, this time successfully.

Now at last he was free to pursue what he had come to feel was the only possible path for him: painting.

ON PROBATION

Gifted with exceptional spirit of mind and with an instinct capable of capturing in his drawings the most characteristic and immediate external aspects — qualities that were already clear in his childhood sketches — Lautrec underwent a long and hard apprenticeship, determined to master all the secrets of painting. In March 1882, he returned to Paris and began to work at Princeteau's studio, at 223 Faubourg Saint-Honoré. A few months later, he joined the atelier of Léon Bonnat, one of the best-known painters of fashionable Paris. There he remained until the end of the year, when Bonnat closed his atelier once and for all.

In the following year, he joined the studio of Fernand Cormon, a painter also very much in fashion at the time. Cormon's academic painting *Cain*, inspired by Victor Hugo, had caused a sensation at the 1880 Salon. Henri remained with Cormon for two years, making friends with many of his fellow disciples (Henri Rachou, René Grenier, Eugène Boch, Charles Laval, François Gauzi, and Louis Anquetin). His affair with Marie Charlet helped him to forget a youthful love for his cousin Jeanne d'Armagnac.

Between 1881 and 1883, Toulouse-Lautrec painted many portraits, mainly using people in his family environment as models: a young peasant (*Young Routy at Céleyran*), his master (*Portrait of the Artist René Princeteau*), and his mother (*The Artist's Mother, Reading in the Garden*). Indeed, Countess Adèle frequently consented to sit patiently for her son, and few other artists have paid homage to their mothers in such a large number of paintings. In *The Artist's Mother*, for instance, Henri proved how skillfully he could communicate a thoughtful moment at a table in a café. In 1883, Countess Adèle bought the castle at Malromé, near Bordeaux, where Lautrec was to spend the last few weeks of almost every summer after his vacation at the seaside.

His art was far from the academic qualities of official or "approved" styles. Indeed, his admiration was directed towards the Impressionists, in particular Degas, and to Japanese art, revealed to him by the many

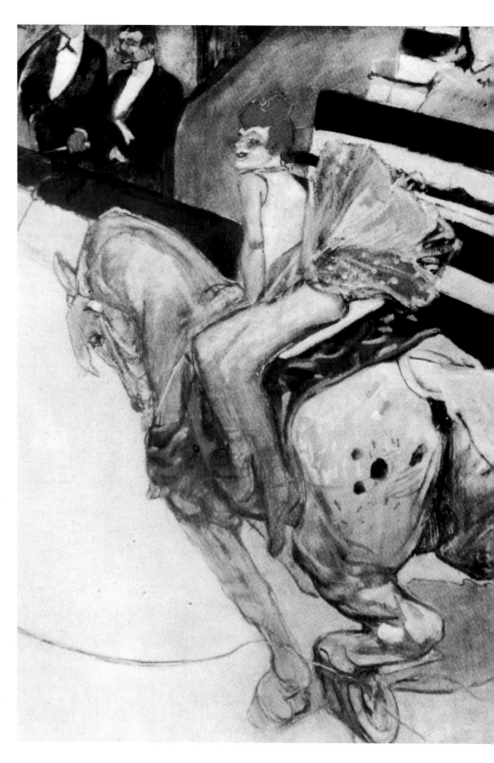

*Horsewoman
at the Fernando Circus*
(detail)

14

Japanese prints to be seen in Paris. In 1884, after leaving Cormon's atelier, he opened his own studio, together with René Grenier, at 19 Rue Fontaine (Edgar Degas's atelier was in the front part of the same building). Sometime later, he went to live with Henri Rachou, at 22 Rue Ganneron. Finally, he moved in with François Gauzi at 7 Rue Tourlaque.

It was in this period that he began to move further away from classical art. The style of his work matured gradually, thanks to his contacts with the new and revolutionary experiences offered by the French capital. The objectivity with which Degas tackled and investigated the everyday life of the suburbs and the glittering world of theatrical shows, the precision and incisive nature of his line and color, the daring formal simplification of the Japanese masters, the elegance of their linear rhythms, the novelty of their compositions — all struck Lautrec to the core. He found among them the basic tools that, once developed, he needed to portray the only thing that aroused passion in him: human reality in its most genuine and unconventional aspects.

In Pau he took part in a collective exhibition organized by several young artists. He painted *The Fat Marie* (also known as the *Venus of Montmartre*), and the portraits of Carmen Gaudin, a beautiful red-headed model. From 1885 on, he also began to patronize the nightclubs of the district, from the Elysée Montmartre to the Moulin de la Galette; but most of all Le Mirliton, the cabaret run by Aristide Bruant, whom he befriended and on whose premises he exhibited some of his works. In the same year, he went to stay with the Anquetin family in Etrepagny and visited Villeneuve-sur-Morin as a guest of the Grenier family. He painted *Portrait of the Painter Emile Bernard* and a portrait of Suzanne Valadon, whom he had just met in Paris. With Suzanne, model and artist (and mother of Utrillo), he was to have a turbulent affair, which ended in her attempted suicide.

In 1886, he spent the summer months at Malromé and at Arcachon, and started to publish drawings in newspapers and magazines such as *Courrier Français*, *Le Mirliton*, and *Paris Illustré*. He also met and became friends with Vincent van Gogh, later painting a portrait of van Gogh of great intensity.

NIGHTLIFE
Henri was now able to follow the path he had chosen for himself, and from this point on, his life, although full of lively episodes, followed an unchanging course.

In the bohemian district of Montmartre, among the nightclubs, the brothels, dance halls and cafés, lived a mixed crowd of people enjoying life to the full, though on the margins of Parisian society. Here at last Toulouse-Lautrec found his world; the place where it was easiest for him to fit in, where even his deformity seemed to go unnoticed and where the frenzied and apparently carefree life constantly provided him with stimulus for his curiosity and inspiration for his restless art. He made friends with actors and actresses and went to see reviews and plays. Everywhere, he tried to reach and capture the most genuine and essential side of the human character; to seize it in the frenzy of a dance, in the freedom of gestures protected by the intimacy of an alcove, or in the magic revelation of a theatrical show. In 1887, he went to live with Henri Bourges at 19 Rue Fontaine, and opened a studio on the fourth floor of 27 Rue Caulaincourt, on the corner of Rue Tourlaque, where he remained until 1897.

He took part in collective exhibitions in Toulouse, under the pseudonym of "Tréclau" (an anagram of Lautrec). He also painted the *Pastel Portrait of Van Gogh*, as well as *At the Masked Ball at the Elysée Montmartre*, and the first of his interiors of the Moulin de la Galette, of which the one portraying La Goulue and Valentin le Désossé is the most famous.

In 1888 he took part in an exhibition in Brussels with the group of artists dubbed the "Vingts." Vincent van Gogh's brother Theo took some of Henri's canvases to store them for the Boussod & Valadon gallery. The artist himself spent the autumn in Villiers-sur-Morin. He painted a number of portraits, as well as cabaret and circus scenes — including the famous *Horsewoman at the Fernando Circus*. Although this painting clearly revealed some Japanese influence, it pinpointed the original style of this young artist. It already contained some important elements of that style: the absence of shadows, the diagonal lines of the composition, the special cut of the painted figures and certain decorative arabesques. The colors were pure and were spread as a wide background with free and vigorous brushstrokes, the result of long hours of preparation.

In the following year, he began to exhibit paintings in Paris at the Salon des Indépendants (this was to become a regular event for him until 1894) and at the Cercle Artistique et Littéraire in the Rue Voleny. In the garden of "Père" Forest, a Montmartre photographer, he painted a series of portraits. He then spent the summer in Arcachon, where, sadly, a hunter killed Tom, a tame cormorant Henri had grown fond of.

Model in the Artist's Studio:
Hélène Vary

Nevertheless, he was not too upset and won boat races at the helm of Damrémont's yacht.

Dance halls were a powerful attraction for Toulouse-Lautrec. His preference in this period was for the Moulin de la Galette, a cabaret in an old windmill in Montmartre. This nightclub had enjoyed long-lasting and vast popularity in the past. In 1876 Renoir had painted its garden. Henri, instead, painted the interior. This was the famous *Au Moulin de la Galette*. In the foreground there are several women awaiting their escorts, behind them a man in a hat, and in the background the chorus girls milling to and fro while a group of people stand talking.

Then on October 5, 1889, the Moulin Rouge was opened. Lautrec became a regular, and his *Horsewoman at the Fernando Circus* hangs in the entrance hall to this day. Here he was to spend much of his brief and intense life. All his works from this period are recognizable by their distinctive characteristics: the cutting aggressiveness of the brushstrokes, with their exceptional force of expression; the audacity of the compositions; and the violence, but never cruelty, with which the vices and weaknesses, the physical and spiritual features of humanity are revealed.

In 1890, he went to Brussels with Paul Signac and Maurice Guibert for the inauguration of the exhibition of the "Vingts." There he quarreled with De Groux, whom he challenged to a duel to defend the work of Van Gogh. On July 6, the Dutch painter was Lautrec's guest in Paris and his former school friend Maurice Joyant took the place of Theo van Gogh (who had suffered a stroke) as the manager of the Goupil gallery. Lautrec painted *La Danse au Moulin Rouge*, which Oller, Zidler's partner in the nightclub, immediately bought and placed above the bar (where it remained until 1893). Compared with *The Dance at the Moulin de la Galette*, painted in 1889, this later painting has a more complex composition: the depth of the room is suggested by the superimposition of human figures placed on various levels. In the midst of the customers who watch them are La Goulue and Valentin le Désossé, two cabaret stars who, thanks to Lautrec, found a place in the history of art. At this time he met the singer Jane Avril and began to paint a series of beautiful portraits of her, such as the famous poster showing her sitting at the Divan Japonais, a café-cabaret at 75 Rue des Martyrs. For a time, he lived in the high-class brothel in the Rue des Moulins, and enjoyed showing up at gala evenings at the opera with its madame, Marie-Victorine Denis.

Between 1889 and 1890 he painted *Justine Dieuhl Sitting in the Forest Garden*. Then, in 1891, he moved with Bourges to the house next door (21 Rue Fontaine). Lautrec's favorite cousin, Gabriel Tapié de Céleyran, came to Paris to study medicine, and it was in this period that Lautrec painted Doctor Péan performing an operation. He then took part in a collective exhibition at the Barc de Boutteville, a characteristic rendezvous in the Rue Pelletier, which earned him critical praise.

Lautrec painted *A la Mie*, the subject and atmosphere of which are reminiscent of Degas's *Absinthe*, painted in 1876. In *A la Mie*, Lautrec shows the interior of a tavern, where a couple are seated at a table. The characters of the two are rendered perfectly, showing the euphoria of the drunken man and the bad temper of the red-headed woman, who is almost turning her back on her companion.

THE MOULIN ROUGE

On joining the club La Revue Blanche, Toulouse-Lautrec made many friends, particularly the Natanson brothers. It was at their home that he met, among others, Vallotton, Bonnard and Vuillard. With them, at La Revue Blanche, Lautrec discovered the cultural atmosphere of Art Nouveau. It was a style particularly favorable for applied art forms such as *affiches*, or posters, drawing its inspiration from the lithographs covering the walls of Paris and filling the pages of avant-garde magazines. During the course of 1891, he began to produce lithographs. The first *affiche* to bring him fame was the *Moulin Rouge (La Goulue)*.

In 1892, he exhibited works at the 8th Salon des Indépendants, at the "Cercle" in Rue Volney, at the Barc de Boutteville, and in Brussels with the "Vingts" group. But Lautrec was still attracted to the nightlife of Montmartre, since it represented the source, so to speak, of his inspiration. To the arrogance of his own social class it seemed that he preferred the natural qualities of the people who came to Montmartre. In this respect *L'Anglais au Moulin Rouge*, painted in 1892, may be considered an indirect form of self-portrait. As a man of aristocratic lineage, he was well aware of the lust concealed behind the polite façades of so-called men of the world. In *Jane Avril Leaving the Moulin Rouge*, painted in the same year, Lautrec showed the singer coming out of the Moulin Rouge, deep in thought, leaving the multicolored bustle of the nightclub behind her. Her sensible clothes, dark and ladylike, contrast with the garish colors of the surrounding environment. It is a skillful rendering of the intimate contrast between inner thought and the outer world, and almost a declaration of love to a woman whom

*Justine Dieuhl Sitting
in the Forest Garden*

20

only Lautrec really understood. These two beings, so different physically, had in common the same sense of melancholy.

By this time the Moulin Rouge had become an obsession with Lautrec, and he returned to the same theme throughout the whole year.

Au Moulin Rouge is a sizable composition that Lautrec enlarged further and corrected at a later stage by adding new parts. It shows a different part and view of the nightclub: its *promenoir*. The painting, on canvas, is one of his most carefully executed works. Alongside a diagonally drawn parapet, customers of the nightclub — three men and two women — can be seen talking at a table; on the right, in the foreground, the light strikes violently upon the face of a woman (Jane Avril?) dressed in dark clothes. In the background, La Goulue, together with another woman, tidies her hair in the mirror while Lautrec, in a bowler hat, and his lanky cousin and friend Gabriel Tapié de Céleyran cross the room behind her.

In *Au Moulin Rouge: Start of the Quadrille*, the subject is a dancer, perhaps La Goulue herself, taking up her position for the dance, with her skirts raised, while in the foreground a couple, who have clearly only just arrived, cross the dance floor looking for somewhere to sit. The dancer's expression and the positions of her arms and legs, which portray unmistakably the start of a quadrille, convey simultaneously annoyance for the interference and the pleasure she takes in her role. Here, Lautrec captured with masterly skill a specific instant that, in the sparkling shimmer of the colored lights, a less sensitive eye would have been unable to see. He captured the moment as in a photograph and made it eternal by transforming it in art. As in many of his other oil paintings, the technique was characterized by economy: the shades of orange were achieved mainly by leaving the cardboard support unpainted so that its natural hue remained.

Also in 1892, together with Bonnard, Lautrec created artwork for the advertisements for a new novel published by Victor Hugo, *Reine de Joie*. Bonnard created the cover, the quality of which was poor, while Lautrec prepared the poster, his second important work in this genre. It shows a *cocotte* sitting at the table of a restaurant, kissing a bald, stout man on the nose. Here again, as in Lautrec's first poster, there is a return to Japanese *cloisonné* work. The play on surfaces and contours is shown up effectively by relatively few chromatic emphases.

In Lautrec's posters and other graphic printing works, one has to make a clear-cut distinction between the written words executed by the artist himself, and the subsequent overprinting by the customer at the time of printing the poster, generally done without the artist's contribution. Only the wording by Lautrec is of any artistic interest, although it is not always up to the same standards of the painting. This applies to the *Reine de Joie*, where the letters are irregular, seeming to tremble a little, and are not of the same heights and thicknesses; they might almost have been fashioned by a child's hand. Yet the purpose of the artist can be sensed by intuition: to integrate the wording into the style of the drawing, to achieve unity of the letters and image. His intention was not always fully realized, but the poster of the *Moulin Rouge* is certainly the best example.

In 1893, Lautrec left Jane Avril for Yvette Guilbert, although he remained good friends with the singer. In this same year, he painted Jane many times: seated, from the front, from the back, wearing gloves, dancing, as an onlooker, and leaving the Moulin Rouge.

In February, Joyant organized a personal exhibition for Lautrec at the Boussod & Valadon gallery. It was quite successful, and the exhibition earned the approval of the great Degas. Lautrec also took part in the "Vingts" exhibition in Brussels once again. In the meantime, he moved into his mother's flat in the Rue Douai and drew the poster for the Jardin de Paris, a nightclub which opened on May 7.

"There Is Nowhere Else I Feel More at Home"

As was customary among the artists of the time, he lived and painted in a high-class brothel in the Rue d'Amboise, where he had a short affair with "La Grande Mireille." He did sixteen paintings for the salon, oval medallions showing a woman's head, surrounded by flower decorations in an eighteenth-century style, in keeping with the good taste of the madame, Blanche d'Egmont.

Around this time he painted *Louis Fuller at the Folies-Bergères*, a study for the lithograph with the same name, and *Monsieur, Madame and the Puppy*, portraying a couple of brothel owners. In this period, it was in brothels that he painted his best nude studies, the most genuine portraits, the consequence of an intimacy that had become daily habit and was therefore devoid of both complacency and contempt. Any subject, even the trickiest, seemed to flow pure from the brushes of Lautrec. Rather than judging or condemning, he salvaged every human attitude and made it authentic. In the same year he took part in the 5th Exposition des Peintres-Graveurs with twelve lithographs.

He felt a profound attraction for the theater, too, and he worked on posters and programs for plays, as well as dedicating paintings and lithographs of famous actors and actresses. His friend Tristan Bernard introduced him to the world of sport, where he also found new interests and new excitements.

In 1894 he left for Brussels, where he took part in the Salon de la Libre Esthétique (which had taken over from the Groupe des Vingts). He also visited Bordeaux — and London, where he met Oscar Wilde. On May 15, he took part in an exhibition of avant-garde artists in Toulouse and painted *Living in a Brothel* and *In the Salon in Rue des Moulins*.

The latter is the most important of the works in which Lautrec drew his inspiration from the lives of prostitutes. A thick, enveloping atmosphere, emphasized by the purplish shades of the color, prevails throughout the large room; and the stiff figure of the *maîtresse*, calmly waiting to receive the customers, stands out among the "girls" reclining on the sofas. He captured perfectly the facial expressions and the different poses taken up by the women as they wait. In *The Sofa*, the theme is the same: two "girls" rest after their day's work. Lautrec was fascinated by the natural spontaneity of the prostitutes. He was able to win their confidence and thus could observe them undisturbed in their own environment. While living in one of these houses, he aroused the indignation of some visitors by asking them to come to see him at home in the brothel. One of these was the art dealer Paul Durand-Ruel.

Although Lautrec loved this kind of joke, the most important reason for his place of residence was undoubtedly of an artistic nature. It was only by becoming closely acquainted with the daily life of prostitutes that he could illustrate the reality of their lives, without embellishing or falsifying it. As with his paintings of the cabaret world, he had first of all to acquire direct experience of what he intended to paint. Here were the characters of whom the artist was able to identify and capture the most personal and significant traits. This he did with an increasingly acute and accurate analysis, showing their integrity with his strong graphic technique and his unpredictable, ingenious use of colors. Lautrec often purposely made the faces and bodies uglier than they actually were, as if he were able to look inside them. Yet, at the same time, he made them so human that they seem almost pure. It was a kind of catharsis that induced the onlooker to be less inclined to make hurried judgments. There was neither disgust nor pleasure, merely the description of a "natural state."

YVETTE GUILBERT

Lautrec produced a large number of drawings, gouaches and lithographs of Yvette Guilbert. When she met the artist, Yvette was already a famous singer (after a tour in America in 1893 she became even more famous). She had the peculiarity of wearing a pair of very long black gloves, and this is how Lautrec painted her. In this respect the paintings *Yvette Guilbert's Black Gloves*, *Yvette Guilbert Greeting Her Audience* and *Yvette Guilbert as a Reciter*, all dated 1894, are typical. There was also a plan for a poster of Yvette. Unfortunately this was never produced, probably because the star, used to being more flatteringly portrayed by other artists, was too hesitant to entrust this task to Lautrec. Several letters written by the singer in 1894 show clearly how shocked she was by the way Lautrec saw and depicted her: "...For the love of God, do not make me so atrociously ugly! A bit less..." In the end, however, Lautrec's art persuaded her and one can say without doubt that Guilbert owes her immortality solely to the works of Lautrec. The artist also made two sets of black-and-white lithographs of the singer. The first of these albums was published in Paris in 1894, and included a text by the art critic Gustave Geffroy. Some have been published separately, without the written text. The second album appeared in 1898 in London (and therefore belongs to the "English series"). In the latter, Lautrec included a larger number of close-ups of this prima donna, mostly just her face or half-length portraits. The first album, in contrast, had shown the "Guilbert phenomenon" as her whole silhouette.

"THEM" (ELLES) AGAIN

In 1894 he painted a series of pictures showing the "girls" of the luxury Parisian brothel in Rue des Moulins. *The Salon in the Rue des Moulins* was his most demanding composition inspired by this theme, a daring, non conformist painting that embodies a courageous and sincere political vocation. He continued to work at a feverish pace, alternating paintings and posters with humorous drawings for newspapers, illustrations for books, and color lithographs.

In the summer of 1895, he traveled from Bordeaux to Lisbon by sea, meeting the subject for *The Passenger from Cabin 54*, as the subsequent painting was entitled, thus rendering immortal an unknown traveler with whom he had fallen in love.

In the same year, he provided the decorations for La Goulue's fairground booth, posters for May Milton, and also for May Belfort, with whom he had an affair. He also took part in a number of collective exhibitions. In January 1896, he held an exhibition at Goupil's gallery — and for the Paris publisher Gustave Pellet he prepared an album of color lithographs, *Elles*, which, however, did not sell well. *Elles* was centered on the daily lives of prostitutes in their brothels. This series, already revolutionary by its theme, was even more so in the extremely refined use of the lithographic technique. Here, rather than the strong and contrasting colors of his posters which were aimed at catching the attention of the observer, Lautrec chose delicate intermediate tones (e.g., *The Bathtub*). The gradation of the surface textures is enriched by hatchings and spray effects consisting of tiny dots. The album was definitely a milestone in the history of color lithography.

Lautrec visited Bordeaux, Lisbon, Madrid and Toledo, and spent the autumn in Arcachon. Twenty-one of his posters were exhibited at the Cirque de Reims in an exhibition of Affiches Artistiques, Françaises et Etrangères, Modernes et Rétrospectives. In the winter he was back in Paris, but he spent the end of the year in London.

He produced the poster for the Simpson bicycle chain, and also drew *Chocolat Dancing in the Irish and American Bar*. This drawing shows the colored male dancer Chocolat performing an elegant, feline dance in the Irish and American Bar. Like the bony and macabre silhouette of Valentin le Désossé, this character, with his almost monkey-like exoticism, is one of Lautrec's few male portrayals that remain fixed in the memory alongside his innumerable female characters.

DELIRIUM
Unfortunately, Lautrec began to suffer from increasingly severe mental disturbances, tremors and bouts of amnesia, and he began to experience the typical hallucinations of an alcoholic. On May 11, 1897, he moved his studio to 15 Rue Frochot. Early in the summer, he went to Holland with Maxime Dethomas, then to Villeneuve-sur-Yonne, where he had an attack of delirium tremens during which he shot at imaginary spiders with a revolver. This was the year of the *Nude in Front of the Mirror* and *Trip to the Country*.

In 1898 he held a large personal exhibition at Goupil's London gallery. As a result of his declining health, his productivity decreased in quantity, but not in quality. The second collection of lithographs of Yvette Guilbert (nine etchings) came out in London. In the autumn, he

Au Moulin Rouge:
the Promenoir
(detail)

returned to Paris, where he had another bout of alcoholism, and came to believe that he was being persecuted by the police.

He started to illustrate Jules Renard's *Histoires Naturelles*; and in 1899, following a fit, he spent three months in the "Madrid" nursing home for mental diseases in Neuilly. Thereupon, a controversial press campaign was launched against Lautrec, and he was even declared mad. To prove to the doctors that he had recovered, he painted from memory a series of circus scenes, and at last regained his freedom, going for a period of rest to Le Havre, then to Bordeaux, and lastly to Malromé.

The castle of Malromé in Gironde was a refuge where his mother waited for him, ready to take him under her wing in times of crisis. In spite of the continued surveillance of his friend Paul Viaud, he resumed drinking large quantities of alcohol. The pictorial style of Paris and Bordeaux was clearly visible in *Miss Dolly from the Star at Le Havre* (1899), in *The Jockey* (1899) and in the *Rat Mort* (1900). His monochromatic lithograph *The Jockey* exists in several versions, colored by hand by Lautrec using different tones. The violence of the colors used added even further to the expressive force of the motif of the two jockeys moving rapidly away on horseback. This work is almost superior to the paintings on a similar theme by Degas, and also represents one of the greatest peaks of Lautrec's production.

In the *Rat Mort* restaurant scene, beside a companion who is barely shown and whose profile is cut short by the right edge of the canvas, we can see a garishly dressed woman seated at a table. In front of her, in the forefront, a still-life type study of fruit occupies the left part of the picture. With her affected, doll-like appearance, the *cocotte* seems to become part of these decorations, her face similar to one of the pieces of fruit, ready to be tasted. The vivid red of her heart-shaped, painted lips and the yellow of her face can also be found in the pear in the fruit bowl. The painting is based not only on the contrast between light and dark areas, but also — for the first time — on the presence of almost variegated surfaces, structured solely by their colors.

A la Toilette would appear to have been painted in 1898. In it, the gaze of a young prostitute (Mme. Poupoule) in her mirror seems to have so much more richness of content than all the various portraits at dressing tables painted by Renoir and Degas. Lautrec contributes some deeper meaning to this theme, making it seem as if it had been treated with superficiality by other artists. Observed close up, the composition and the melancholic content are reminiscent of his early self-portrait.

Chocolat Dancing in the
Irish and American Bar
(detail)

28

As in a circle that is closing, here again is a still-life study arranged in the forefront, on the makeup table. It is a moment of introversion interrupting a daily activity, the woman's glance turned towards the mirror. As with the *Nude in Front of the Mirror* of 1897, the painting is no celebration of beauty and eroticism. Indeed, it reflects their inevitably transitory nature. These female subjects seem to be asking questions such as: "Who am I? What will become of me? What is the meaning of all this?"

The Final Work

In 1900 Lautrec quarreled with his family over financial matters. He held exhibitions in Paris and Bordeaux, where he became a theatergoer (six paintings were inspired by *Messalina*). After a long summer spell at the seaside, Lautrec spent the winter at Malromé. An infection left his lower limbs paralyzed, but he managed to recover.

Starting in mid-April 1901, Lautrec spent three months in Paris, concentrating assiduously on his work. On August 15, in Taussat, he was struck by paralysis, and on August 20 he was taken to Malromé, where he painted a few more canvases. On September 9, at only thirty-seven — the same age as Raphael — he died in the arms of his mother. He was buried originally in Saint-André-du-Bois, but his body was later moved to Verdelais (Gironde). His last works were *Examination at the Faculty of Medicine* and *Admiral Viraud*.

Life Is Art

Like Gauguin and Van Gogh, Toulouse-Lautrec is one of those artists for whom it is impossible to separate the art from the painter's life. Not only does he not have a definite place in the history of art, but he was also the object of protests on the part of those who saw in him nothing more than a very capable poster artist. Moreover, his artistic evolution is not easily identified.

From the fine watercolors of his adolescence, he passed almost in a single leap to the great topic of his artistic maturity: people. Certainly, neither Princeteau nor Bonnat nor Cormon, who were excessively academic painters, can help us understand this great leap towards a personal art characterized by movement and light. Indeed, Lautrec's knowledge of academic concepts led him towards a more opaque and less free way of using color. His encounter with the works of Degas definitely left a mark; and the same can be said for Japanese art. Yet

Portrait of Gabriel
Tapié de Céleyran

30

Lautrec's light differs from any other light. It is not the warm, life-giving light of the sun, but the pale and cold light of gas lamps and lightbulbs.

Many feel that Lautrec was basically a draftsman, even when he painted. Indeed, none of his paintings are modeled on color alone. He used a special technique even in his oil paintings, in order to retain the rapidity and lightness of a drawing. He diluted his colors with turpentine, which, being extremely volatile, dries quickly, and with this mixture he would paint on absorbent cardboard. Gray cardboard was not just the support on which he painted; it also became itself an element of the composition. The origins of many of his "color drawings" did not lie merely in his turpentine-based paints, but also in a mixture of pencils and watercolors or simply pastels, as in 1890, while he was at the Neuilly nursing home. He rarely used another medium. Both the portrait of Van Gogh of 1887 and the *Barmaid in London* of 1898 are pastels.

Lautrec cannot be classed as belonging to any specific artistic group or movement. He had a strong aversion for everything that was theory and doctrinal. For practical reasons, he is often numbered among the Impressionists, but this is a mistake and a rather superficial idea. There is, in fact, an aspect that separates him from the latter: his love for the city, for intimate and small spaces. Landscapes did not attract him much, while for the Impressionist painters these were the main inspiration, if not the only theme. For Lautrec, they were merely an accompaniment, almost an ornament.

What attracted his interest, and took up practically the whole space of the picture, were human figures. These allowed him to exploit his gift as an observer. His tense and nervous brushstrokes, his qualities as a colorist, were to be the instruments of a basically bitter, almost implacable, psychological investigation. He remained faithful to the elementary rules of perspective, although at times, through Degas, he did take the full liberty of distorting space. The characters he illustrated were depicted as if the observer were actually another of the actors in the scene being described. The observer was placed upon the same plane. Thanks to this expedient, the observer has the feeling of being an active participant, as if he actually belonged to what is going on. In *Dance Moresque*, painted in 1895, one of the panels decorating La Goulue's Booth, Lautrec used close-ups. Because of the different proportions he gave the characters, he was able to place the spectator among the crowd intent on watching the bedeviled dance. In *Jane Avril Leaving the Moulin Rouge*, on the other hand, the spectator has the feeling of having just come across her in the livid light of the avenue. Lastly, in the *Dance at the Moulin Rouge*, he almost becomes the escort of two young women crossing the dance floor.

Lautrec's fame as a draftsman is unmistakably linked to his graphic work, an activity in which he reached the apex of his effectiveness. What is more, he appreciated this so well himself that his painting was changed by it. He began to use vigorous and overlapping planes and simple colors with great effect. His arabesques stretch like springs, and seem to tear the surface.

Lautrec understood the power and usefulness of the poster, and how its effectiveness depended on the speed of perception. The more surprising a poster, the more the unconscious mind of the passerby is able to take in the image, and this is immediately associated with the product that it advertises. The effect on the tranquil passerby of Lautrec's first posters, standing out against the gray walls of Paris, certainly had the impact of a fanfare. They were the first notes of a splendid symphony, to be expanded on by others early in the twentieth century.

Over and above any moral judgment, the portrayal of Lautrec's day and age, which he handed down to us through his art, is one of the most acute, fascinating and revealing that any artist has ever painted. The work of this artist, however, cannot be understood without investigating the social framework of the period known as *fin-de-siècle*. For Toulouse-Lautrec, it was, in the end, the brief space of a painful and yet deeply involved inquiry into existence.

Self-Portrait

Young Routy at Céleyran

Portrait of the Artist's Mother at Breakfast

(Portrait of) Jeanne Wenz

Portrait of Suzanne Valadon

Dancing at the Moulin de la Galette: La Goulue and Valentin le Désossé

A Corner of Moulin de la Galette

The Woman with Gloves (Portrait of Honorine P.)

Mademoiselle Dihau at the Piano

Moulin Rouge

(Moulin Rouge) La Goulue

Woman Sitting in a Garden

In the Moulin Rouge

Une Redoute au Moulin Rouge

Two Women Waltzing

Two Women Waltzing (detail)

Au Moulin Rouge: La Goulue et sa Soeur

Reine de Joie

Aristide Bruant dans son Cabaret

Aristide Bruant at Les Ambassadeurs

Confetti

Poster for the Divan Japonais

Jardin de Paris: Jane Avril

Jane Avril Dancing

La Loge

La Loge (detail)

Yvette Guilbert Greeting Her Audience

Loie Fuller

The Salon in the Rue des Moulins

The Sofa

May Belfort

Woman Putting on Her Stockings (Woman of the House)

Marcelle Lender Dancing the Bolero in Chilpéric

Marcelle Lender Dancing the Bolero in Chilpéric (detail)

Portrait of Oscar Wilde

Napoleon

May Belfort (lithograph)

May Milton

The Clownesse Cha-Wo-Kao

Cha-Wo-Kao (dans sa loge)

Women in the Dining Room (Les dames au réfectoire)

May Belfort

Woman in a Corset from "Elles"

Woman at Her Toilet

Woman at Her Toilet (detail)

La Chaîne Simpson (poster)

Femme au Tub

Study for a Box at the Theater

At the Bar, the Client and the Cashier

The Jockey

Jane Avril

The Sphinx

The Private Room at the Rat Mort at Cabinet

The Englishwoman at "The Star"

Messalina Descending the Staircase

Madame Poupoule at Her Dressing Table

Examination at the Faculty of Medicine